LE CORDON BLEU
HOME COLLECTION
·VEGETABLES·

MEREHURST

contents

recipe ratings ✸ *easy*   ✸ ✸ *a little more care needed*   ✸ ✸ ✸ *more care needed*

Vegetable pot-au-feu

A healthy, energising dish that won't spoil your figure!
Simple to make and very satisfying.

Preparation time **35 minutes**
Total cooking time **1 hour 20 minutes**
Serves 6

STOCK
500 g (1 lb) chicken wings, chopped,
    or wing tips
300 g (10 oz) carrots, roughly chopped
1 leek, roughly chopped (see page 63)
2 celery sticks, roughly chopped
1 onion, halved
2 cloves, inserted into the onion
1 bay leaf
3 sprigs of fresh thyme

300 g (10 oz) carrots, cut into 5 mm (¹/4 inch) cubes
300 g (10 oz) turnips, cut into 5 mm (¹/4 inch) cubes
500 g (1 lb) potatoes, cut into 5 mm (¹/4 inch) cubes
220 g (7 oz) green beans, topped
    and tailed
90 g (3 oz) frozen baby peas
ground white pepper
2 tablespoons chopped fresh chervil

1 To make the stock, put the chicken wings or tips in a saucepan and cover with about 3 litres of water. Add the chopped carrot, leek, celery, onion halves and cloves, bay leaf and sprigs of thyme. Bring slowly to the boil, then reduce the heat and simmer for about 50 minutes. Skim frequently to remove any froth from the surface of the stock.

2 Pass the stock through a fine sieve. If possible, line the sieve with a piece of muslin cloth or a coffee filter to obtain a clear liquid. Discard the chicken, vegetables, herbs and spices.

3 Cook the carrot, turnip and potato in boiling salted water for 2–3 minutes, or until tender but still crunchy. Plunge into cold water to stop the cooking process and keep the vegetables crunchy.

4 Cut the green beans into six pieces and cook in boiling salted water for 4 minutes. Drain, plunge into cold water to stop the cooking process and retain the green colour, then drain again. Add the baby peas to boiling salted water and cook for 1 minute. Drain, plunge into cold water, then drain again.

5 Season the stock with salt and white pepper, to taste. Add all the vegetables and reheat. Serve very hot in a soup dish and sprinkle with the chervil.

Rösti

A Rösti can be made from potatoes that have already been cooked, making a quick and delicious dish.

Preparation time **15 minutes**
Total cooking time **40 minutes**
Serves 6

500 g (1 lb) floury potatoes
oil, for cooking
25 g (3/4 oz) unsalted butter
1 onion, thinly sliced

1 Preheat the oven to moderate 180°C (350°F/Gas 4). Scrub the unpeeled potatoes and put them in a saucepan. Cover with cold water, add salt, and bring to the boil. Reduce the heat and simmer for 10 minutes. Drain and allow the potatoes to cool completely.
2 Peel the potatoes and either cut them into very fine sticks or coarsely grate them. Do not rinse.
3 In a non-stick ovenproof frying pan, heat a little oil and add the butter. Gently cook the onion until soft and transparent. Add the potato, season with salt and pepper, mix for a few minutes, then press down with the back of a spoon or wide spatula to form a thick flat pancake. Brown one side over medium to high heat and transfer the pan to the oven for 15 minutes. Loosen and tip the pancake over onto a large plate and then slide it off the plate and back to the pan browned-side-up. Be careful not to break the potato, and mind your fingers as there may be some loose hot oil and butter. Return to the oven and bake for another 10 minutes. For serving, cut into slices like a cake.

Artichokes with blue cheese

Tender artichoke bottoms or hearts are the most delicious part of this vegetable. Stuffing them with a blue cheese purée makes them extra special.

Preparation time **20 minutes**
Total cooking time **20 minutes**
Serves 4

6 artichoke bottoms, cooked (see page 62)
30 g (1 oz) blue cheese, crumbled
2 heaped tablespoons fresh breadcrumbs
50 g (1 3/4 oz) unsalted butter, melted

1 Preheat the oven to moderately hot 200°C (400°F/Gas 6). Rinse the cooked artichokes under cold water and set four aside.
2 Cut the remaining two artichokes into cubes and place in a food processor. Process with the crumbled blue cheese until smooth, then season with freshly ground black pepper. Spoon into the four artichoke bottoms, forming the purée into a dome. Place in a baking dish.
3 In a small bowl, mix the breadcrumbs and half the butter together and sprinkle on top. Drizzle with the remaining melted butter and bake for 20 minutes, or until golden brown. In the picture, the artichokes are garnished with watercress.

Chef's tip If you cannot get fresh artichokes large enough for this recipe, good-quality preserved or canned ones work very well.

Crisp mushroom and chestnut pastries

*A delicious combination of mushrooms and chestnuts with a light creamy sauce in crisp buttery pastry.
Serve as a first course or a light luncheon dish accompanied by a salad.*

Preparation time 20 minutes + refrigeration
Total cooking time 40 minutes
Serves 4

400 g (12³/4 oz) ready-made puff pastry
1 egg, beaten
470 g (15 oz) mixed, wild mushrooms (see Chef's tip)
clarified butter (see page 63) or oil, for cooking
2 French shallots, finely chopped
1 clove garlic, crushed
juice of ¹/2 lemon
30 ml (1 fl oz) dry Madeira
**60 g (2 oz) can whole unsweetened
   chestnuts, roughly chopped**
30 g (1 oz) chopped fresh parsley
125 ml (4 fl oz) thick (double) cream

1 Preheat the oven to hot 220°C (425°F/Gas 7). Roll the pastry to a rectangle about 5 mm (1/4 inch) thick. With a large sharp knife, trim to straighten the two long sides and cut two long strips, 7 cm (2³/4 inches) wide. Now cut two diamonds from each strip, with the vertical side 7 cm (2³/4 inches) long. Place the four diamonds slightly apart on a damp baking sheet and refrigerate for 20 minutes.

2 Brush the top surface with beaten egg. Do not brush the side edges as the egg will set and prevent the pastry from rising. Bake for 15 minutes, or until crisp and golden brown. With a sharp knife, split the diamonds in two horizontally. Scrape out any soft dough and discard. Keep the pastry pieces warm.

3 To prepare the mushrooms, wash them two or three times, drain and cut into bite-sized pieces. Heat a little clarified butter or oil in a large frying pan and fry the mushrooms until golden brown. Drain, reserving the juices. Meanwhile, heat a little butter in a frying pan and cook the shallots for 2–3 minutes. Add the garlic, lemon juice, Madeira, chestnuts and parsley. Season with salt and pepper.

4 Pour the mushroom juices into the shallot mixture and simmer, uncovered, until the liquid is reduced by half. Add the cream and season with salt and pepper. Reduce the sauce over high heat for 10 minutes, or until it is a syrupy consistency. Toss the mushrooms in the sauce and spoon into the bottom half of the pastry. Arrange the pastry lid on top and serve.

Chef's tip Oyster, shiitake, chanterelle, cloud ear, pied de mouton or pied bleu are all suitable mushrooms. Use one type or a mixture. If wild mushrooms are not available, use cultivated mushrooms, washing only once.

Potato and spinach croquettes

The humble, indispensable potato is enhanced with the flavours of spinach and Parmesan in these popular delights.

Preparation time **30 minutes**
Total cooking time **45 minutes**
Makes 14 croquettes

500 g (1 lb) floury potatoes
pinch of ground nutmeg
20 g (³/4 oz) unsalted butter
1 egg yolk
oil, for deep- or shallow-frying
40 g (1 1/4 oz) Parmesan, freshly grated
50 g (1³/4 oz) cooked English spinach, finely chopped
60 g (2 oz) plain flour, seasoned with salt and pepper
3 eggs, beaten
1 tablespoon peanut (groundnut) oil
150 g (5 oz) dry breadcrumbs

1 Cut the potatoes into similar-sized pieces for even cooking, by halving or quartering, depending on their size. Put in a saucepan, cover with cold water and add a large pinch of salt. Bring to the boil, lower the heat and cook for at least 20 minutes, or until quite tender.

2 Drain the potatoes and dry them by shaking them in the pan over low heat for 2 minutes. Press them through a sieve or finely mash them until smooth. Season with salt and pepper, to taste, and nutmeg. Add the butter and egg yolk. Spread out on a tray to cool. Preheat oil in a deep-fryer or large pan, to moderate 180°C (350°F). The oil will be hot enough when a cube of bread browns in 15 seconds.

3 Mix the Parmesan with the very well-drained spinach in a bowl. Add the potato, salt and pepper to this mixture and stir to combine. On a floured surface, and using floured hands, roll the mixture beneath a flat hand to form cylinders about 6 x 2 cm (2¹/2 x ³/4 inches). Even up and flatten the ends.

4 Place the seasoned flour on a tray. Combine the eggs and oil in a bowl and put the breadcrumbs on a large piece of greaseproof paper. Roll the croquettes carefully through the flour and pat off the excess. Dip them in the egg to coat thoroughly, drain off the excess and roll in the breadcrumbs, lifting the edges of the paper to make it easier. Sometimes it is necessary to coat the croquettes twice in the egg and crumbs. Do this if your mixture is a little too soft to hold its shape well. Fry in batches until evenly browned and lift out, shaking off any excess oil. Drain on crumpled paper towels.

Chef's tips The potato must not be too wet as the croquettes will split and absorb the oil.

Shake off or press on excess breadcrumbs or they will burn and cling to the croquettes as unsightly specks.

Mediterranean-style roasted capsicums

This colourful, tasty dish is suitable for serving as a first course or using as a side dish with seafood, meat or chicken.

Preparation time **10 minutes + 3–4 hours marinating**
Total cooking time **10–15 minutes**
Serves 6

1 red capsicum (pepper)
1 green capsicum (pepper)
1 yellow capsicum (pepper)
2 teaspoons capers, finely chopped
4 anchovy fillets, finely chopped
3 tablespoons fresh basil leaves, shredded
80 ml (2³/4 fl oz) olive oil

1 Cut all the capsicums in half, remove the seeds and membranes and put the cut capsicums on a grill tray cut-side-down.

2 Brush the capsicums with a little oil and cook under a preheated grill until the skin has blackened and blistered. Cover with a tea towel or enclose in a plastic bag and allow the capsicums to cool. The skins will then come away from the flesh more easily.

3 Remove the skins, cut the flesh into thick strips and put them in a bowl.

4 Place the capers, anchovies and basil in a jug, stir in the olive oil and pour the mixture over the capsicums. Season, to taste, with salt and pepper. Marinate in the refrigerator for 3–4 hours before serving. Serve with focaccia and a green salad.

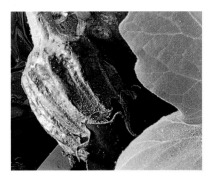

Eggplant caviar

The name of this dish comes from the rather grainy appearance of the eggplant.
Delicious served with crisp Melba toast or warmed pitta bread.

*Preparation time **10 minutes + 1 hour refrigeration***
*Total cooking time **30 minutes***
Serves 6

❀

800 g (1 lb 10 oz) eggplants (aubergines)
50 g (1³/4 oz) pitted black olives, chopped
1 clove garlic, crushed
4 tablespoons finely chopped fresh chives
155 ml (5 fl oz) olive oil
¹/2 teaspoon paprika

1 Preheat the oven to moderate 180°C (350°F/Gas 4). Cut the eggplants in half lengthways. Brush the cut sides with a little olive oil and sprinkle with salt and pepper.

Bake for 25–30 minutes, or until the flesh is very soft.
2 Drain the eggplants to remove any liquid. Scrape out the flesh with a spoon, chop the flesh and put in a bowl.
3 Add the black olives, garlic and half the chives. Mix everything together using a fork, squeezing the eggplant flesh against the sides of the bowl to break it down. Add the olive oil very slowly, stirring it into the mixture with the fork. Add the paprika and season, to taste, with salt and pepper. Refrigerate for 1 hour.
4 Spoon into a chilled bowl, sprinkle the top with the reserved chives and serve with Melba toast.

Chef's tip For a special presentation, use two spoons to shape the mixture into small quenelles and arrange on individual plates. Sprinkle with chopped chives.

Braised red cabbage

The French name for this northern dish, an excellent accompaniment to roast pork or game, is Chou rouge à la flamande. Slow-cooking produces a wonderful result.

*Preparation time **20 minutes***
*Total cooking time **1 hour 45 minutes***
*Serves **8***

I red cabbage
45 g (1 1/2 oz) unsalted butter
I onion, sliced
2 cooking apples
2 tablespoons white wine vinegar
I tablespoon sugar
I 1/2 tablespoons plain flour

1 Preheat the oven to warm 170°C (325°F/Gas 3). Quarter the cabbage, cut out and discard the stalk and shred the cabbage finely. Put the cabbage in a large saucepan of boiling salted water (there should be enough water to more than cover the cabbage), bring back to the boil and drain. The cabbage will now have taken on an inky blue colour. This is normal, and it will regain its colour later. You may have to do this in batches, depending on the size of the saucepan.

2 Melt 15 g (1/2 oz) of the butter in a large casserole, add the onion, cover and cook gently until transparent. Peel, quarter, core and slice the apples finely before adding them to the onion. Cook for a few minutes, remove the mixture from the dish and set aside.

3 Add the cabbage to the casserole, layering with the onion and apple mixture and sprinkling with the vinegar, sugar and 2 tablespoons of water. Season with salt and pepper. You will see the red colour return as the vinegar is added. Cover with thickly buttered paper and the lid and bake for about 1 1/2 hours, or until very tender. Stir occasionally and moisten with a little extra water if necessary.

4 Soften the remaining butter in a bowl and mix in the flour. Push the cabbage to one side of the pan. There will be some liquid at the bottom of the casserole. Add one quarter of the butter and flour and stir in. The liquid will thicken slightly. Repeat on the other side. Toss together and only add more butter and flour if any watery liquid is present. A lot of flavour and seasoning is in the liquid, so it is just thickened to cling to the cabbage. Do not thicken too much. Taste and season. The cabbage should be gently sweet and sour. It may be necessary to add a little more sugar or vinegar, to taste.

Little stuffed vegetables

*Master the preparation of these delightful, elegant vegetables so you and
your friends can savour the results.*

*Preparation time **45 minutes***
*Total cooking time **1 hour***
Serves 4

125 g (4 oz) fresh breadcrumbs
170 ml (5¹/₂ fl oz) milk
olive oil, for cooking
125 g (4 oz) lean pork, minced
125 g (4 oz) lean veal, minced
3 cloves garlic, finely chopped
1 egg yolk, lightly beaten
2 tablespoons chopped fresh parsley
4 small turnips, about 5 cm (2 inches)
  in diameter
1 large zucchini (courgette), at least 21 cm
  (8¹/₂ inches) in length, ends removed
2 large potatoes, peeled

1 Preheat the oven to moderately hot 200°C (400°F/
Gas 6). Mix the breadcrumbs and milk in a large bowl
and set aside while you cook the meat. In a large frying
pan, heat a little olive oil and cook the pork, veal and
garlic for 5 minutes over medium heat. Remove from

the heat and mix into the bread and milk. Season, to
taste, and add the egg and parsley. Set aside.

2 Peel the turnips and slice off the tops and bottoms,
leaving the vegetables 4 cm (1¹/₂ inches) high with a
4–5 cm (1¹/₂–2 inch) diameter. Use a melon baller to
scoop the flesh out. Discard the flesh, leaving a border
1 cm (¹/₂ inch) thick on the sides and bottom. Cut the
zucchini into lengths, about 4 cm (1¹/₂ inches) each,
and scoop the flesh out, as with the turnips.

3 Cut the potatoes into 4 cm (1¹/₂ inch) cubes and,
using a 4 cm (1¹/₂ inch) round cutter, cut the potatoes
into round tubes. Scoop out the centre as for the other
vegetables. Blanch each vegetable in a separate pan of
boiling water, being careful not to overcook any of
them. They should remain firm. Transfer the turnips and
zucchini to a bowl of iced water and, when completely
cooled, place upside down on paper towels to drain.
When the potatoes are cooked, put them on paper
towels, right-side-up, until cool enough to handle.

4 Season the interiors of the prepared vegetables and
spoon the filling into them. Place the filled vegetables in
a lightly oiled ovenproof dish and brush with a little
olive oil. Bake for 20–30 minutes, or until just tender. If
desired, brown under a grill. Serve hot or cold.

Vegetable strudel

*A delightful start to a meal or perfect as a light luncheon dish. A slight hint of curry flavour
enhances the lightly cooked vegetables in crisp pastry.*

*Preparation time **40 minutes***
*Total cooking time **1 hour***
Serves 4–6 (Makes 10)

oil, for cooking
1 onion, chopped
1/2 teaspoon mild curry powder
450 g (14 1/4 oz) mixed peeled vegetables,
    such as finely diced carrot, parsnip, turnip
    and celeriac; French beans, cut into short
    lengths; one quarter each of a cauliflower
    and a broccoli, cut into tiny florets; a small
    leek, finely sliced (see page 63)
2 tablespoons fresh breadcrumbs
20 sheets filo pastry
oil or melted butter, for brushing

TOMATO AND CORIANDER SAUCE
15 g (1/2 oz) unsalted butter
1 onion, finely sliced
450 g (14 1/4 oz) tomatoes, peeled, seeded and
    quartered (see page 62)
    or 400 g (12 3/4 oz) can tomatoes
60 ml (2 fl oz) vegetable or chicken stock
    (see page 63)
1 bay leaf
1 sprig of fresh thyme
3 tablespoons chopped fresh coriander leaves

1 Preheat the oven to moderately hot 190°C (375°F/
Gas 5). Heat a little oil in a sauté pan or wok and gently
fry the onion until just soft. Add the curry powder and
blend in. Add the carrot, parsnip, turnip and celeriac
and toss for 2 minutes over high heat. Add the beans,
cauliflower and leek and toss for another minute before
adding the broccoli and frying for 2 minutes. Transfer to
a large bowl, lightly mix in the breadcrumbs and season
with salt and pepper, to taste.

2 Brush one sheet of filo pastry with oil or melted
butter and place another sheet on top before brushing
again with oil or melted butter. Fold in half and scatter
on the vegetables, leaving 2.5 cm (1 inch) on each side
free of filling. Turn these sides in and roll up the strudel
carefully. Repeat this process until all the filo pastry and
vegetables have been used. Transfer the strudels to a
lightly buttered baking tray and gently brush the pastry
with oil or melted butter. Bake for 15–20 minutes, or
until crisp and golden brown.

3 To make the tomato and coriander sauce, melt the
butter in a pan, add the onion and cook for 10 minutes
until transparent. Add the tomato, stock, bay leaf and
thyme, and season with salt and pepper. Bring to the
boil, reduce the heat, cover and simmer for up to
20 minutes, or until rich and pulpy. (If using canned
tomatoes, add with the juice and, when soft, remove the
lid and cook to reduce until thick.) Remove from the
heat. Discard the bay leaf and thyme, add the coriander
and season, to taste. A pinch of sugar may be required if
the tomatoes are sharp. Serve the strudels immediately
with the tomato and coriander sauce.

Chef's tips The strudels should be served as soon as they
are cooked, otherwise the pastry may go soft. If you
prefer, prepare the strudels a few hours ahead and brush
again with melted butter just before baking.

This is an excellent recipe to use up small amounts of
fresh vegetables in your refrigerator. Be careful not to
use vegetables that will become watery and make the
pastry soggy, such as zucchini (courgettes). If using up
cooked vegetables, dice them and mix in after cooking
the onion, but do not cook further.

Roasted parsnips with honey and ginger

A very popular vegetable in Ancient Greece and during the Middle Ages and the Renaissance, the parsnip has a lovely sweet flavour.

Preparation time **10 minutes**
Total cooking time **20 minutes**
Serves 6

6 parsnips, about 750 g (1¹/₂ lb)
60 ml (2 fl oz) oil
15 g (¹/₂ oz) unsalted butter
1 tablespoon clear honey
1 tablespoon finely grated or chopped fresh ginger

1 Preheat the oven to hot 220°C (425°F/Gas 7). Cut the peeled parsnips in half lengthways, or quarters if they are large, to make pieces about 8 cm (3 inches) long and 2.5 cm (1 inch) thick. Remove any woody cores. Put in a large pan and cover with water. Add a pinch of salt and bring to the boil over high heat. Boil for 1 minute before draining. Return to the saucepan and dry well by shaking the pan over low heat for about 1 minute.

2 Heat the oil in a roasting pan on the stove. Add the parsnips and cook quickly over high heat, turning to colour evenly. Add the butter to the pan, transfer to the oven for 10 minutes. Spoon or tip out the excess oil.

3 Add the honey and ginger, turning the parsnips to coat evenly, and roast for another 5 minutes.

4 Lift the parsnips out of the pan and serve hot with pork or chicken.

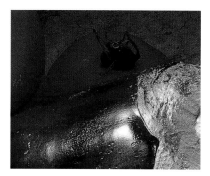

Baked eggplant

The pronounced flavour of the eggplant is often combined with tomato, garlic and herbs.
These stuffed eggplants originated in Turkey as Imam bayildi.

*Preparation time **40 minutes***
*Total cooking time **1 hour***
Serves 4

olive oil, for cooking
2 large French shallots, finely chopped
800 g (1 lb 10 oz) tomatoes, peeled, seeded
   and diced (see page 62)
6 cloves garlic, finely chopped
small pinch of cayenne pepper
60 g (2 oz) fresh basil leaves, chopped
2 small eggplants (aubergines)
4 small tomatoes, stems removed
100 g (3¹/4 oz) Gruyère or Swiss cheese, grated

1 Preheat the oven to slow 150°C (300°F/Gas 2). In a heavy-based frying pan, heat a little oil over medium heat, add the shallots and cook for 2–3 minutes, without colouring. Add the diced tomato and garlic, season with salt and cayenne pepper and simmer for 15 minutes, or until thick. Mix in the chopped basil, set aside and keep warm.

2 Meanwhile, cut the eggplants in half lengthways. Score the flesh, being careful not to cut through the skin. Rub the surface with olive oil and season with salt. Place the eggplant cut-side-down in an ovenproof dish or roasting pan and bake for 15 minutes, or until soft. Allow to cool. Increase the temperature of the oven to moderately hot 200°C (400°F/Gas 6).

3 Cut the small tomatoes in half from top to bottom and thinly slice into semicircles. Set aside.

4 Carefully scoop out the flesh of the cooked eggplant. Set the empty skins aside. Chop up the pulp and remove some of the liquid by cooking in a frying pan for 5–10 minutes over low heat. Transfer the eggplant pulp to a bowl and mix in half of the cooked tomato. Season and then spoon the mixture into the eggplant skins. Put the filled eggplants in an ovenproof dish and arrange the tomato slices on top. Sprinkle with the grated cheese and bake until golden brown.

5 Purée the remaining cooked tomato in a blender. Thin out if necessary with some water or chicken stock. Place in a small saucepan and heat through, checking the seasoning. To serve, spoon some of the tomato sauce onto the plate and arrange the eggplant on top.

Cauliflower cheese

Perfect partners, cauliflower and cheese baked in this way make a hearty winter dish that never has the experience of being a leftover.

Preparation time **10 minutes**
Total cooking time **30 minutes**
Serves 4–6

1 whole cauliflower, about 470 g (15 oz)
   when trimmed
30 g (1 oz) unsalted butter
30 g (1 oz) plain flour
500 ml (16 fl oz) milk
pinch of ground nutmeg
100 ml (3¼ fl oz) cream
130 g (4¼ oz) Gruyère cheese, grated
2 egg yolks

1 Preheat the oven to moderate 180°C (350°F/Gas 4). Remove the outer leaves of the cauliflower and break the head into small serving-sized pieces. Place in cold salted water, bring slowly to the boil, reduce the heat and simmer for about 10 minutes, or until the cauliflower is cooked, but still slightly firm. Drain, refresh in cold water, then drain again.

2 To make the cheese sauce, melt the butter in a pan, stir in the flour with a wooden spoon or whisk and cook over low heat for 3 minutes. Remove from the heat and gradually stir in the cold milk. Return to the heat and bring to the boil, stirring continuously. Add the nutmeg and season with salt and pepper. Stir in the cream. Remove from the heat and add 100 g (3¼ oz) of cheese and the egg yolks. Set aside. Cover the surface with plastic wrap or damp greaseproof paper to prevent a skin from forming.

3 Lightly brush an ovenproof dish with butter. Pour a thin layer of the sauce onto the base, arrange the cauliflower on the sauce and pour over the remaining sauce so that it coats the cauliflower. Sprinkle with the remaining cheese and some pepper and nutmeg and bake for 15 minutes, or until the cheese is golden brown.

Chef's tips If the sauce looks lumpy before the cream has been added to it, simply whisk it until smooth. It is important to do this before the cheese is added to prevent strands of cheese from sticking to the whisk.

Gruyère is a strong cheese, but if you use a different type with less strength, add a little mustard to bring out the flavours.

Asparagus with hollandaise sauce

Before World War I, hollandaise sauce was called Sauce Isigny, after a town in Normandy known for its butter. During the war, butter production came to a halt and it was imported from Holland. The name was changed to hollandaise to indicate the source of the butter and was never changed back.

*Preparation time **45 minutes***
*Total cooking time **35 minutes***
Serves 4

HOLLANDAISE SAUCE
3 egg yolks
200 g (6¹/2 oz) clarified butter, melted
  (see page 63)
small pinch of cayenne pepper
juice of ¹/2 lemon

32 asparagus spears
4 tablespoons rock salt

1 To make the hollandaise sauce, whisk the egg yolks with 3 tablespoons of water in a medium heatproof bowl until foamy. Put the bowl over a larger pan of simmering water and continue whisking over low heat until the mixture is thick and you can see the trail made by the whisk. Remove from the heat and gradually add the butter, whisking constantly. Once all the butter has been incorporated, strain the sauce and season with salt, to taste, a dash of cayenne pepper and the lemon juice. Keep the sauce warm over a pan of warm water. (If preferred, a food processor can be used to make the sauce. Whisk the egg yolks and water and, with the motor running, add the melted warm butter to the processor in a thin stream.)

2 Bring a large pan of water to the boil. Use a vegetable peeler to remove the outer layer from the lower two thirds of the stem of each asparagus spear. Line up the spears of asparagus and tie into bundles of eight.

3 Add the rock salt and then the asparagus bundles to the water. Reduce the heat and simmer for 10 minutes, or until the tips are tender. Remove and drain on paper towels. Remove the string and arrange each bundle on a warm plate. Coat with some of the hollandaise sauce and serve immediately.

Chef's tip Hollandaise sauce is an emulsion sauce like mayonnaise, but made with warm clarified butter, which helps to make a smooth sauce. Once made, the sauce should be kept lukewarm. If the sauce is overheated, it will separate. If this should happen, the sauce can be repaired by adding a little cold water and whisking.

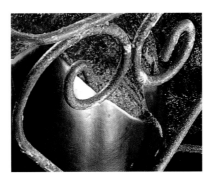

Ratatouille

This is a classic dish from the sunny area of Provence using the freshest tomatoes, zucchini, eggplants, capsicums and onions, sautéed in olive oil with herbs.

*Preparation time **40 minutes***
*Total cooking time **1 hour***
Serves 4

❁ ❁

1 onion, diced
80 ml (2³/4 fl oz) olive oil, for cooking
250 g (8 oz) tomatoes, peeled, seeded
*   and chopped (see page 62)*
2 cloves garlic, chopped
1 red capsicum (pepper), seeded and cut
*   into short strips*
bouquet garni (see Chef's tips)
250 g (8 oz) zucchini (courgettes), cut
*   into batons (see page 63)*
250 g (8 oz) eggplants (aubergines), cut
*   into batons*
60 g (2 oz) chopped fresh basil leaves

1 Preheat the oven to moderate 180°C (350°F/Gas 4). In an ovenproof frying pan, cook the onion in a little of the olive oil, over medium-low heat, for 3–5 minutes, or until soft, being careful not to let the onion colour. Add the tomato and garlic and cook for 15 minutes, stirring occasionally.

2 In another frying pan, sauté the red capsicum in oil for 2–3 minutes over medium-high heat. Strain off the excess oil and add to the tomato mixture with the bouquet garni.

3 Sauté the prepared zucchini and eggplant separately in oil, for 3–4 minutes. Add to the tomato mixture. Season with salt and pepper, to taste, cover and bake for 30 minutes. Just before serving, remove the bouquet garni, stir in the chopped fresh basil leaves and adjust the seasoning, if necessary.

Chef's tips The bouquet garni is a selection of herbs tied in a neat bundle for easy removal from the dish before serving. It is made by wrapping the green part of a leek around celery leaves, a sprig of thyme, a bay leaf and parsley stalks, and then securing them together with string. When using a herb such as basil in the recipe, you can replace the parsley stalks with the basil stalks for added flavour.

This dish can be made on the stove top instead of being baked. Cook over low heat, stirring often.

Provençal stuffed tomatoes

Olive oil, garlic, parsley and tomato predominate in the cuisine of the Provence region, reflecting its close proximity to Italy.

Preparation time **30 minutes + 20 minutes draining**
Total cooking time **15 minutes**
Serves 4

4 tomatoes
60 ml (2 fl oz) extra virgin olive oil
4 cloves garlic, finely chopped
1 tablespoon chopped fresh thyme leaves
2 tablespoons chopped fresh parsley
60 g (2 oz) fresh breadcrumbs

1 Preheat the oven to moderately hot 190°C (375°F/Gas 5). Remove the stem ends from the tomatoes. Place the tomatoes stem-side-down (to make the tomatoes more secure) and cut in half. Carefully remove the seeds with a teaspoon. Season with some salt and leave, cut-side-down, on paper towels to drain for about 20 minutes.

2 Gently heat the olive oil until warm. Remove from the heat and add the garlic, thyme, parsley and breadcrumbs. Season with salt and pepper and mix well using a wooden spoon. Season the tomato halves with pepper and fill with the bread stuffing, making a slight dome on top of each tomato half. Place in an oiled ovenproof dish and drizzle with some extra olive oil. Bake for 5–10 minutes, or until the stuffing is golden.

Chef's tip This recipe would also work successfully using eight small tomatoes with the tops cut off and the seeds scooped out.

Mixed glazed vegetables

*This colourful, attractively prepared mixture of vegetables looks very appealing presented
at the table in a shallow dish.*

*Preparation time **40 minutes***
*Total cooking time **30 minutes***
Serves 4

20 pearl onions
2 zucchini (courgettes)
3 turnips
3 carrots
60 g (2 oz) unsalted butter
3 teaspoons sugar

1 Soak the pearl onions in a bowl of warm water for 5 minutes, to make peeling easier. Lightly trim the root end, being careful not to cut off too much, since it is the root end that will keep the pearl onions intact.
2 Using a standard 2 cm (3/4 inch) melon baller, make 20 balls each of the zucchini, turnip and carrot. Cook the zucchini balls for 1 minute in boiling salted water and refresh in iced water. Drain and transfer to a small saucepan. Add one third of the butter, 1 teaspoon of the sugar, 1/2 teaspoon salt and 30 ml (1 fl oz) water and cook until the water has evaporated and a syrupy glaze remains. Check to see if the vegetables are tender. If not, add some water and cook a little longer. Roll the vegetables around to evenly coat, then set aside and keep warm.
3 Put the turnip and carrot balls together in a pan with half of the remaining butter, 1 teaspoon of the sugar, 1/2 teaspoon salt and enough water to just cover. Cook in the same way as the zucchini, then set aside and keep warm. Repeat with the peeled pearl onions.
4 Reheat by combining the vegetables in a pan, placing the pan over medium heat and rolling the vegetables around to prevent them from browning, for about 3–5 minutes. Transfer to a serving dish.

Chef's tips Leave the vegetables at room temperature for about 1 hour before preparing.

If you can't get pearl onions, use small pickling onions and remove a few outer layers.

Chickpea and sesame fritters with garlic and olive sauce

Chickpeas feature in many dishes in the south of France, as well as in the Middle East and Spain.
These fritters team well with the garlicky flavour of the sauce.

*Preparation time **55 minutes + 30 minutes soaking***
*Total cooking time **2 hours***
Makes 20

❂ ❂

170 g (5¹/2 oz) dried chickpeas
80 ml (2³/4 fl oz) sesame oil
2 eggs, beaten
125 g (4 oz) sesame seeds
oil, for deep-frying

GARLIC AND OLIVE SAUCE
¹/2 head of garlic, separated into cloves
   and peeled
15 g (¹/2 oz) unsalted butter
¹/2 onion, chopped
200 ml (6¹/2 fl oz) milk
50 ml (1³/4 fl oz) cream, optional
100 g (3¹/4 oz) black olives, chopped

1 tablespoon chopped fresh flat-leaf parsley or
   fresh coriander leaves, optional

1 Soak the chickpeas in warm water for 30 minutes. Drain, cover well with fresh water in a deep pan and simmer for about 1¹/2 hours, or until soft.

2 Drain the chickpeas and while hot, purée them in a food processor until fine. Slowly incorporate the sesame oil. Season with salt and pepper, to taste.

3 Roll the mixture into balls about the size of a dessertspoon. Dip them in the beaten egg and coat with the sesame seeds. Heat the oil to moderate 180°C (350°F), and deep-fry the balls in batches until golden. Drain on paper towels and keep warm.

4 To make the garlic and olive sauce, gently sauté the garlic in the butter until golden brown. Add the onion and cook until the onion is just soft but without colour. Add the milk, bring to the boil and cook for 10 minutes. Purée the mixture in a blender, add the cream, and salt and pepper, to taste. Strain the sauce and add the chopped black olives.

5 Place three or four of the chickpea fritters per person on plates and pour the garlic and olive sauce around them. Sprinkle with the chopped fresh parsley or coriander leaves and serve immediately.

Vegetable tian

Layers of vegetables with added flavour from herbs and garlic are delicious baked in a shallow dish that can be presented at the table. Suitable for lunch or dinner.

*Preparation time **30 minutes***
*Total cooking time **1 hour***
Serves 4

olive oil, for cooking
I small onion, thinly sliced
750 g (1 1/2 lb) tomatoes, peeled, seeded
  and diced (see page 62)
400 g (12 3/4 oz) large mushrooms, thinly sliced
400 g (12 3/4 oz) potatoes, thinly sliced
2 cloves garlic, finely chopped
500 g (1 lb) English spinach leaves,
  stems removed
I sprig of fresh rosemary
3 tablespoons chopped fresh parsley

1 Preheat the oven to moderately hot 190°C (375°F/Gas 5). In a heavy-based pan, heat a little olive oil over medium heat and gently cook the sliced onion with a pinch of salt for 3 minutes, without allowing to colour. Add the seeded and diced tomato and cook gently for 7 minutes. Season, to taste, and set aside.
2 Pan-fry the mushrooms in a little olive oil over high heat for 3–4 minutes. Drain off any excess moisture. Season, to taste, and set aside.
3 Pan-fry the potato in batches in some olive oil, over medium-low heat for 3 minutes. Return all the potato to the pan, add the garlic and cook for another minute. Season with salt and freshly ground black pepper and drain on paper towels.
4 Arrange a layer of potato in the bottom of a 2-litre capacity, 20 cm (8 inch) diameter round or oval ovenproof dish and cover with a layer of the mushrooms followed by a layer of spinach, then tomato. Bake for 30–45 minutes, covered with greaseproof paper. Sprinkle with rosemary leaves and parsley before serving.

Chef's tip If desired, cover the vegetables with grated Parmesan or crumbled feta cheese before baking.

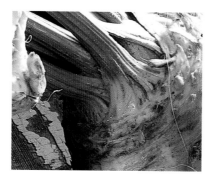

Celeriac rémoulade

This is a delicious first course or can be served as a light lunch, perhaps with chunks of bread.
The mustardy mayonnaise enhances the crunchy celeriac's unique taste.

*Preparation time **40 minutes***
  + 30–60 minutes resting
*Total cooking time **Nil***
Serves 4–6

❀

2–3 celeriac, total weight about 1.3 kg (2 lb 10 oz)
juice of 1 lemon
several small salad leaves, to garnish
2 tomatoes, peeled, seeded and diced
  (see page 62), to garnish
walnut halves, to garnish

REMOULADE SAUCE
2 egg yolks
2 tablespoons Dijon mustard
pinch of cayenne pepper
250 ml (8 fl oz) peanut (groundnut) oil

1 Using a large knife, cut each celeriac in half and peel away the skin, cutting about 3 mm (1/8 inch) deep under the skin (the skin is very fibrous so it is important to cut off enough). Coarsely grate the celeriac and put the flesh in a bowl. Season with salt and pepper and toss in the lemon juice. Cover with plastic wrap and set aside for 30–60 minutes.

2 To make the rémoulade sauce, in a medium bowl, whisk together the egg yolks, mustard, cayenne pepper and a pinch of salt. Once the salt has dissolved, gradually whisk in the oil. The sauce should resemble stiff-peaked whipped cream.

3 Squeeze out the excess liquid from the shredded celeriac and mix the celeriac with the sauce. Season with salt and freshly ground black pepper, if necessary. Serve the rémoulade in a large bowl or in small domes on individual plates, decorated with the salad leaves, tomato and walnut halves.

Stuffed cabbage

This is an excellent luncheon or supper dish. In some countries, cabbage is not regarded as a vegetable suitable for serving as a separate course, but the following is definitely worthy of being offered in this way.

*Preparation time **45 minutes***
*Total cooking time **1 hour 35 minutes***
Serves 6

1 green cabbage, about 500–800 g (1 lb–1 lb 10 oz)
60 g (2 oz) unsalted butter
1 small onion, finely chopped
120 g (4 oz) fresh breadcrumbs
4 tablespoons chopped fresh parsley
1 tablespoon chopped fresh thyme leaves
grated rind of 1/2 lemon
2 eggs, beaten
15 g (1/2 oz) clarified butter (see page 63)

1 Trim off any tired cabbage leaves, but leave the cabbage whole. Plunge it into a large pan of boiling water. Boil for 3–4 minutes. Tip off the hot water, transfer the cabbage to a colander and drain well. Allow to cool slightly. Carefully detach four to six outside leaves and set aside. Cut the cabbage into quarters, remove the stalk, then slice the cabbage and chop finely.

2 Melt the butter in a large pan, add the onion, cover and cook gently for 1–2 minutes. Add the cabbage, press a piece of buttered paper on the top, cover the pan and cook over low heat for 25–30 minutes, stirring thoroughly once or twice during cooking. The cabbage should be soft and golden all through. Draw aside, stir in 90 g (3 oz) of the breadcrumbs, the herbs, lemon rind and eggs, and season with salt and pepper.

3 Line a large pudding basin with a buttered piece of muslin or clean cloth. Arrange the reserved outside leaves in this, stalks uppermost. Fill with the mixture, gather the ends of the cloth tightly, twist and tie the cloth to give the cabbage a plump shape. Lift out of the basin, and plunge the cabbage into a pan of boiling salted water or vegetable stock. Boil gently and steadily for 45 minutes to 1 hour. Turn it over once or twice during cooking. Lift out into a colander, drain well, untie the cloth and turn the cabbage over onto a hot dish.

4 Melt the clarified butter in a small pan, add the remaining breadcrumbs and fry until golden. Sprinkle over the cabbage and serve at once with a tomato sauce or well-seasoned passata poured around.

Green beans with bacon

Very popular as a vegetable on the side, served with grilled or baked meats or chicken.
The salty flavour of bacon blends perfectly with green beans.

*Preparation time **10 minutes***
*Total cooking time **15 minutes***
Serves 4–6

500 g (1 lb) green beans
1 teaspoon salt
300 g (10 oz) smoked bacon
50 g (1³/4 oz) unsalted butter
3 tablespoons finely chopped fresh parsley

1 Top and tail the beans. Bring a large saucepan of water to the boil. Add the salt and the beans and simmer for 10 minutes, or until tender. Drain and refresh with cold water to stop the cooking process. Drain well.
2 Meanwhile, remove the rind from the bacon and discard. Cut the bacon into small, short strips. Heat a frying pan, add the bacon and fry over medium heat.

There is no need to add any fat, the bacon's own fat will melt into the pan as it cooks. Remove the bacon and drain on paper towels.
3 Drain the excess fat from the pan, wipe with paper towels and then melt the butter in the pan. Toss the beans in the butter, add the bacon and season with salt and pepper. As soon as they are warmed through, transfer to a serving dish, sprinkle with chopped parsley and serve.

Chef's tips To maintain the green colour of the beans, simultaneously throw the salt and the beans into the boiling water. This creates a fast bubble, which helps to fix the chlorophyll.

As a variation, substitute the bacon with two or three tinned anchovy fillets. Prepare them first by soaking in milk, draining and then drying them. Finely chop them and toss in the butter.

Gratin dauphinois

This potato dish has many versions, some with onion or other vegetables added, some with stock and different herbs. Seasoning, cheese, cream and garlic are the key to making this particular version successful. Experiment to suit your own taste.

Preparation time **30 minutes**
Total cooking time **1 hour**
Serves 4–6

500 g (1 lb) potatoes
500 ml (16 fl oz) milk
nutmeg, grated
100 ml (3¼ fl oz) thick (double) cream
1 clove garlic, chopped or minced
100 g (3¼ oz) Swiss cheese, grated

1 Preheat the oven to warm 170°C (325°F/Gas 3).
2 Thinly slice the potatoes. Place in a saucepan, cover with the milk and season with some salt, pepper and grated nutmeg.
3 Bring to a simmer over medium-low heat and simmer until the potato is almost cooked but still firm. Strain and set the milk aside.
4 Rub a 20 x 16 cm (8 x 6½ inch) ovenproof dish with some butter. Arrange the potato in even layers in the dish.
5 Reheat the milk and allow to simmer for a few minutes. Add the cream and garlic, bring back to a simmer and check the seasoning. Simmer for a few minutes, then pour over the potato. Sprinkle with the grated cheese and bake for 35–45 minutes, or until the potato is tender and the top is lightly browned.

Chef's tip When making a sauce to accompany a bland vegetable such as potatoes, be sure to season it well.

Vichy carrots

The water used for cooking this dish should really be Vichy water, a natural and healthy mineral water from the springs at Vichy in France. These carrots are a colourful accompaniment to veal and chicken dishes.

Preparation time 15–20 minutes
Total cooking time 20–30 minutes
Serves 4

600 g (1¼ lb) carrots
30 g (1 oz) sugar
60 g (2 oz) unsalted butter
30 g (1 oz) chopped fresh parsley

1 Peel the carrots, slice thinly and put in a pan with enough water to barely cover. Add a pinch of salt as well as the sugar and butter and cover with a paper lid made from a round of greaseproof paper (see Chef's tips).
2 Cook over high heat until almost all the water has evaporated, leaving a syrupy reduction. The carrots should be tender. If not, add a little more water (about 60 ml/2 fl oz) and continue cooking. Toss the carrots to evenly coat them. Sprinkle with the chopped fresh parsley and serve in a deep dish.

Chef's tips The carrots can be cut in different shapes for a more decorative presentation.

A paper lid serves to slow the process of steam escaping, allowing foods to remain moist and prevent them from cooking too quickly. To make a paper lid, prepare a piece of greaseproof paper larger than the diameter of the pan. Fold in half, then in quarters and fold once again into a fan shape. To measure the diameter of the pan, place the point in the centre of the pan and cut at the point the folded paper reaches the edge of the pan. Snip the point and unfold. The paper should now be a circle about the same diameter as the pan with a small hole in the centre.

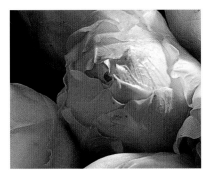

Braised witlof

*A vegetable that is wonderful braised, even though it is often thought
of as being a salad ingredient.*

*Preparation time **15 minutes***
*Total cooking time **1 hour 30 minutes***
Serves 4

60 g (2 oz) unsalted butter
4 witlof (chicory)
500 ml (16 fl oz) chicken stock
  (see page 63) or water
1 tablespoon lemon juice
1/2 teaspoon sugar
1 teaspoon chopped fresh parsley

1 Preheat the oven to moderate 180°C (350°F/Gas 4).
Grease a baking dish with one third of the butter.
Remove any blemished outer leaves of the witlof and
trim and core the root end. This removes some of the
bitterness. Wash and place them in the prepared dish.

2 Add the chicken stock or water with the lemon juice
to the dish. Season lightly with salt, pepper and the
sugar. Bring to the boil on the stove top. Remove and
cover with buttered greaseproof paper and then foil.
Transfer to the oven and bake for about 1–1 1/4 hours, or
until the witlof are tender. Remove the witlof and place
on a rack to drain, reserving the cooking liquid. Cook
the liquid over high heat until syrupy. Set aside and
keep warm.

3 Once the witlof are cooled, lightly tie in the middle
with some kitchen string. Heat the remaining butter in
a non-stick frying pan and brown the witlof until they
are nicely coloured. Remove the string, place the witlof
in a serving dish and cover with the reduced cooking
liquid. Sprinkle with the parsley.

Chef's tip Before tying with the string, you can wrap a
slice of bacon around the middle.

Grilled marinated vegetables

Served cold with a vinaigrette or hot straight from the grill, these vegetables make a delicious light dish, full of colour and flavour.

Preparation time **20 minutes + 2 hours marinating**
Total cooking time **40 minutes**
Serves **6**

1 eggplant (aubergine), about 200 g (6¹/2 oz)
250 g (8 oz) zucchini (courgettes)
200 g (6¹/2 oz) carrots
3 large red capsicums (peppers)
70 g (2¹/4 oz) button mushrooms, washed
2 sprigs of fresh thyme, finely chopped
2 sprigs of fresh parsley, finely chopped
170 ml (5¹/2 fl oz) olive oil
1 tablespoon lemon juice, freshly squeezed
3 tablespoons chopped fresh basil
2¹/2 tablespoons balsamic vinegar

1 Cut the eggplant, zucchini and carrots lengthways into 1 cm (1/2 inch) thick, long slices. Halve the capsicums, remove the seeds and halve into quarters. Remove the mushroom stalks.
2 Spread the vegetables on a tray, sprinkle with salt and pepper, the thyme and parsley. Reserve 2 tablespoons of the olive oil and combine the rest with the lemon juice. Pour over the vegetables and sprinkle with the basil. Marinate for 2 hours.
3 Heat a grill or barbecue and brush with the remaining oil. Slowly grill the vegetables on both sides until tender. (If you prefer less crunchy carrots, grill them for a few minutes before adding the other vegetables.)
4 Arrange the vegetables on a dish and drizzle with the balsamic vinegar.

Vegetable lasagne

Try this deliciously different lasagne with its crunchy vegetables and cheese sauce with a hint of nutmeg. Making your own pasta is both enjoyable and satisfying.

*Preparation time **1 hour + 30 minutes resting***
*Total cooking time **1 hour 30 minutes***
Serves 6

PASTA DOUGH
300 g (10 oz) plain flour
3 eggs, lightly beaten
30 ml (1 fl oz) olive oil
I teaspoon salt

CHEESE SAUCE
25 g (³/4 oz) unsalted butter
25 g (³/4 oz) plain flour
500 ml (16 fl oz) milk
¹/4 teaspoon ground nutmeg
75 ml (2¹/2 fl oz) cream
100 g (3¹/4 oz) Gruyère cheese, grated

25 g (³/4 oz) unsalted butter
I small onion, sliced
4 ripe tomatoes, peeled, seeded
  and chopped (see page 62)
I sprig of fresh thyme
I bay leaf
200 g (6¹/2 oz) carrots, diced
250 g (8 oz) small broccoli florets
¹/2 cauliflower, cut into florets
80 g (2³/4 oz) Gruyère cheese, grated

1 To make the pasta, sift the flour onto a work surface and make a large well in the centre in which to place the eggs, olive oil and salt. Using the fingertips of one hand, mix these together and gradually work in the flour until it is all incorporated. The dough should be slightly dry.

Knead until smooth and silky. Kneading will result in the elasticity and texture required, so don't add extra liquid. Wrap in plastic wrap and rest for 20 minutes.

2 To make the cheese sauce, melt the butter in a pan, stir in the flour with a wooden spoon and cook gently for 3 minutes, stirring continuously. Remove from the heat and whisk in the cold milk. Blend thoroughly, season with salt and pepper and add the nutmeg. Return to the heat and bring slowly to the boil, stirring continuously. Lower the heat and cook for 7 minutes, stirring occasionally. Stir in the cream and cheese. Set aside, covered with buttered greaseproof paper.

3 Heat the butter in a pan and cook the onion slowly without browning. Add the tomato, thyme and bay leaf. Season with salt and pepper. Simmer for 15 minutes, or until pulpy. Discard the bay leaf and thyme.

4 Bring a large pan of salted water to the boil. Add the carrot, reduce the heat and simmer for 4 minutes. Add the broccoli and cauliflower and simmer for 3 minutes. Drain and refresh with cold water to stop the cooking process. Drain well and set aside.

5 Preheat the oven to moderately hot 190°C (375°F/ Gas 5). On a lightly floured surface, roll out the pasta dough to 1 mm (¹/16 inch) thick. Cut with a sharp knife into long strips 8 x 15 cm (3 x 6 inches) and cook a few strips at a time, in a large pan of boiling salted water with a dash of oil, for 2–3 minutes, or until *al dente*. Transfer to a bowl of cold water, drain and put between layers of tea towel.

6 Mix the cheese and tomato sauces and simmer for 15 minutes. Add the vegetables to the sauce. Season. Butter a 2–2.5-litre capacity ovenproof dish and alternate layers of pasta and vegetable mixture, finishing with pasta. Sprinkle cheese over the top and bake for 35 minutes.

Broccoli purée with blue cheese

Puréed broccoli goes well with almost any dish. Add the cheese only moments before serving.

*Preparation time **10 minutes***
*Total cooking time **20 minutes***
Serves 4–6

450 g (14¼ oz) broccoli
40 g (1¼ oz) unsalted butter
45 g (1½ oz) blue cheese, grated or finely crumbled

1 Trim the individual broccoli stalks from the main stem, discard the stem and check that about 220 g (7 oz) of broccoli remains. Wash thoroughly and drain, then trim and slice the stalks very thinly, reserving the flower heads.
2 Melt the butter in a medium pan, add the sliced stalks, cover with greaseproof paper and a lid. Cook very gently for 10 minutes until tender, but not coloured. Finely chop the flower heads and add them to the pan with 125 ml (4 fl oz) water. Cook, uncovered, for 5 minutes until tender, but still bright green. Drain well, transfer to a food processor and blend until smooth. Return to the pan, reheat and remove from the heat to stir in the cheese. Season, to taste, with salt and pepper.
3 Serve the purée as oval quenelle shapes by pushing a rounded dessertspoon of purée off the spoon using another spoon, both held horizontally, or simply serve it in a neat mound.

Chef's tip A great accompaniment to meat, fish or poultry, and especially good with steak. Do not add the cheese until just before serving or it may become stringy with overheating.

Carrot purée

For this method of cooking, the carrots should be sliced very thinly so they will cook quickly and evenly.

*Preparation time **10 minutes***
*Total cooking time **20 minutes***
Serves 4–6

40 g (1¼ oz) unsalted butter
450 g (14¼ oz) carrots, thinly sliced
pinch of nutmeg or ground coriander

1 Melt the butter in a large shallow frying pan, add the carrot and season with salt and pepper. Add the nutmeg or coriander. Cover the pan with a sheet of greaseproof paper and a lid. It is important to cover to prevent loss of steam made by the carrots as they cook, or they will dry and turn brown.
2 Cook over low heat for 15 minutes, or until very soft and tender enough to be mashed with a fork, then remove the paper and lid. Cook, uncovered, over high heat to reduce any excess moisture, then cool slightly. Purée in a food processor until smooth. Return to the pan, adjust the seasoning and reheat to serve. Serve the purée as oval quenelle shapes by pushing a rounded dessertspoon of purée off the spoon using another spoon, both held horizontally, or simply serve it in a neat mound.

Chef's tip The purée may be reheated in the microwave as long as it is in a suitable container.

Carrot purée (top) and Broccoli purée with blue cheese

Warm lentil salad with mustard seed vinaigrette

This traditional regional salad, high in protein, may be served with crustaceans such as prawns. Normally, the small French Puy lentils are used as they hold their shape well. However, other lentils with the same qualities could be substituted for these. Red lentils are not suitable as they soften to a purée.

*Preparation time **15 minutes + overnight soaking***
*Total cooking time **40 minutes***
*Serves **6***

250 g (8 oz) lentils
50 g (1³/4 oz) unsalted butter
100 g (3¹/4 oz) carrots, diced
¹/2 onion, diced
100 g (3¹/4 oz) smoked bacon, diced
300 ml (10 fl oz) chicken stock (see page 63)
I lettuce

VINAIGRETTE
30 g (1 oz) wholegrain mustard
2 teaspoons white wine vinegar
100 ml (3¹/4 fl oz) olive or peanut (groundnut) oil
3 tablespoons chopped fresh parsley

1 Soak the lentils in cold water overnight. Drain.
2 Melt the butter in a large saucepan, add the vegetables and bacon and cook gently until the vegetables are soft, but not brown. Add the lentils and chicken stock to the saucepan. Cover and simmer very gently for 30–35 minutes, or until the lentils are tender. Season with salt and pepper.
3 Pour the mixture into a sieve to drain off the liquid. Transfer the lentils, vegetables and the bacon to a large bowl.
4 To make the vinaigrette, place the mustard and vinegar in a bowl and whisk to combine. Season with salt and freshly ground black pepper and very slowly add the olive or peanut oil, whisking constantly. Finally, add the parsley.
5 Toss the warm lentils, vegetables and bacon with the vinaigrette. Arrange a bed of lettuce leaves on a plate and pile the warm salad in the centre.

Vegetables in white wine

Experiment with different vegetables to see which you prefer. Make this dish according to the traditional recipe below, or vary it with an oriental touch or your favourite herbs.

Preparation time **1 hour**
Total cooking time **50 minutes**
Serves 4

2 tablespoons olive oil
100 g (3¼ oz) bacon, cut into strips
3 French shallots, finely chopped
1 large carrot, cut into batons (see page 63)
1 celery stick, cut into batons
½ fennel root, cut into batons
100 ml (3¼ fl oz) white wine
100 ml (3¼ fl oz) chicken stock (see page 63)
or water
2 large tomatoes, peeled, seeded
and diced (see page 62)
100 g (3¼ oz) shelled fresh peas
100 g (3¼ oz) French beans,
topped and tailed
60 g (2 oz) toasted pine nuts

1 In a large frying pan, heat the oil over medium heat and cook the bacon until golden brown. Lower the heat, add the shallots and a pinch of salt. Cook for 2 minutes, without colouring. Add the carrot, celery, fennel and a pinch of salt, and cook gently for 5 minutes.
2 Add the white wine and chicken stock and cook over medium heat until almost dry. Add the tomato and cook for 5–10 minutes, or until tender.
3 In two separate saucepans, cook the peas and French beans in boiling salted water for 8–10 minutes, or until tender. Drain and refresh in iced water until completely cooled. Drain well and add to the other vegetables. Leave to simmer for 3–5 minutes, or until hot, and season with salt and pepper, to taste. Just before serving, sprinkle with toasted pine nuts. Serve hot or cold.

Chef's tip Slow cooking is a must when preparing this dish, in order to keep it moist. For a more oriental flavour, add toasted sesame seeds instead of the pine nuts and use a little soy sauce instead of salt.

Chef's techniques

◆

Preparing tomatoes

Many recipes call for peeled, seeded tomatoes. It is an easy process if you follow these instructions.

Using a very sharp knife, score a small cross in the base of each tomato.

Blanch the tomatoes in a large pan of boiling water for 10 seconds. Remove and plunge into a bowl of ice cold water to stop the cooking and keep the flesh firm.

Pull away the skin from the cross, and discard the skins.

If a recipe calls for the removal of the tomato seeds, cut the tomato in half and use a teaspoon to gently scoop out the seeds.

Preparing whole artichokes

You can cook either the whole artichoke, as shown below, or just the heart. Both are delicious.

Break off the artichoke stalk at the bottom, pulling out the fibres that attach it to the base.

Pull off the outer leaves and place the artichoke in a pan of boiling salted water with the juice of 1 lemon. Weigh down with a plate and simmer for 20–35 minutes.

Test for doneness by pulling at one of the leaves. If it comes away easily, the artichoke is done. Cut off the top half of the artichoke and discard.

Remove the hairy choke in the middle of the artichoke with a spoon. The artichoke bottom is now ready to fill.

Clarifying butter

Removing the water and solids from butter makes it less likely to burn. Ghee is a form of clarified butter.

To make 100 g (3¹/4 oz) clarified butter, cut 180 g (5³/4 oz) butter into small cubes. Place in a small pan set into a larger pot of water over low heat. Melt the butter, without stirring.

Remove the pan from the heat and allow to cool slightly. Skim the foam from the surface, being careful not to stir the butter.

Pour off the clear yellow liquid, being very careful to leave the milky sediment behind in the pan. Discard the sediment and store the clarified butter in an airtight container in the refrigerator.

Making chicken stock

Good, flavoursome home-made stock can be the cornerstone of a great dish.

Cut up 750 g (1¹/2 lb) chicken bones and carcass and put in a pan with a roughly chopped onion, carrot and celery stick. Add 6 peppercorns, a bouquet garni and 4 litres cold water.

Bring to the boil and let the stock simmer gently for 2–3 hours, skimming off any scum that rises to the surface using a large spoon. Strain the stock through a sieve into a clean bowl, then allow to cool.

Chill the stock overnight, then lift off any fat. If you can't leave overnight, drag the surface of the hot strained stock with paper towels to lift off the fat. Makes 1.5–2 litres.

Baton vegetables

Evenly sized vegetables cook uniformly and look attractive in dishes such as ratatouille.

Use a long, very sharp knife to cut the vegetables into batons.

Washing leeks

Leeks are often used in cooking as they impart a unique flavour.

Before use, leeks need to be rinsed thoroughly under cold running water to dislodge and remove all traces of dirt or grit. Slit the green tops to help the water run through the tightly furled leaves.

Published in 1998 by Merehurst Limited, Ferry House, 51–57 Lacy Road, Putney, London SW15 1PR.

Merehurst Limited, Murdoch Books and Le Cordon Bleu thank the 32 masterchefs of all the Le Cordon Bleu Schools, whose knowledge and expertise have made this book possible, especially: Chef Cliche (MOF), Chef Terrien, Chef Boucheret, Chef Duchêne (MOF), Chef Guillut, Chef Steneck, Paris; Chef Males, Chef Walsh, Chef Hardy, London; Chef Chantefort, Chef Bertin, Chef Jambert, Chef Honda, Tokyo; Chef Salembien, Chef Boutin, Chef Harris, Sydney; Chef Lawes, Adelaide; Chef Guiet, Chef Denis, Ottawa. Of the many students who helped the Chefs test each recipe, a special mention to graduates David Welch and Allen Wertheim. A very special acknowledgment to Directors Susan Eckstein, Great Britain, and Kathy Shaw, Paris, who have been responsible for the coordination of the Le Cordon Bleu team throughout this series.

Managing Editor: Kay Halsey
Series Concept, Design and Art Direction: Juliet Cohen
Editor: Wendy Stephen
Food Director: Jody Vassallo
Food Editors: Lulu Grimes, Tracy Rutherford
Designer: Marylouise Brammer
Photographers: Joe Filshie, Chris Jones
Food Stylists: Carolyn Fienberg, Mary Harris
Food Preparation: Jo Forrest, Kerrie Ray
Chef's Techniques Photographer: Reg Morrison
Home Economists: Michelle Lawton, Kerrie Mullins, Justine Poole, Kerrie Ray

Creative Director: Marylouise Brammer
International Sales Director: Mark Newman
CEO & Publisher: Anne Wilson

ISBN 1 85391 706 0

Printed by Toppan Printing (S) Pte Ltd
First Printed 1998
©Design and photography Murdoch Books® 1998
©Text Le Cordon Bleu 1998

A catalogue record for this book is available from the British Library.

Distributed in the UK by D Services, 6 Euston Street, Freemen's Common, Leicester LE2 7SS Tel 0116-254-7671 Fax 0116-254-4670.
Distributed in Canada by Whitecap (Vancouver) Ltd, 351 Lynn Avenue, North Vancouver, BC V7J 2C4 Tel 604-980-9852 Fax 604-980-8197 or Whitecap (Ontario) Ltd, 47 Coldwater Road, North York, ON M3B 1Y8 Tel 416-444-3442 Fax 416-444-6630
Published and distributed in Australia by Murdoch Books®, 45 Jones Street, Ultimo NSW 2007

The Publisher and Le Cordon Bleu wish to thank Carole Sweetnam for her help with this series.
Front cover, from top: Provençal stuffed tomatoes; Mixed glazed vegetables; Green beans with bacon.

IMPORTANT INFORMATION

CONVERSION GUIDE

1 cup = 250 ml (8 fl oz)
1 Australian tablespoon = 20 ml (4 teaspoons)
1 UK tablespoon = 15 ml (3 teaspoons)

NOTE: We have used 20 ml tablespoons. If you are using a 15 ml tablespoon, for most recipes the difference will be negligible. For recipes using baking powder, gelatine, bicarbonate of soda and flour, add an extra teaspoon for each tablespoon specified.

CUP CONVERSIONS—DRY INGREDIENTS

1 cup flour, plain or self-raising = 125 g (4 oz)
1 cup sugar, caster = 250 g (8 oz)
1 cup breadcrumbs, dry = 125 g (4 oz)

IMPORTANT: Those who might be at risk from the effects of salmonella food poisoning (the elderly, pregnant women, young children and those suffering from immune deficiency diseases) should consult their GP with any concerns about eating raw eggs.